Energy Medicine Principles for Parents:

A Pediatrician's Perspective on How Energy Medicine Can Help Your Child

By Peter Hanfileti, MD

2009

Points of Origin, PLLC & PrinciplesforParents.com

Vancouver, Washington, USA 98684

Published by Points of Origin, PLLC and PrinciplesforParents.com

Printing and distribution through www.lulu.com

First edition, First Printing 2009.

ISBN 978-0-557-13193-8

Printed in the United States of America.

Dedication

I'd like to dedicate this book to the hardest working people I know: *Parents!*

To those parents I have had the pleasure of working with throughout my career, I am especially grateful for the challenges you presented to me. You taught me not to settle for the *status quo* and to continually search for answers, even when we were told there were none. Your unwavering dedication to your children's health, growth, and well-being is an inspiration. Without your courage to find new ways to explain and treat the physical, behavioral, emotional, and mental challenges that children face today, *Energy Medicine Principles For Parents* would not exist.

I would also like to thank my own parents for their love and support throughout my own childhood. You have both helped me understand the wisdom behind the words; *the older I get the smarter my parents get.*

It is my firm belief that the success I have experienced with treating difficult pediatric conditions could not have been achieved without integrating specific energy medicine systems that were compatible with modern medicine. I offer my deep gratitude to Dr John Veltheim for his teaching, mentorship, and ongoing development of *The BodyTalk System*.

And last but not least, I want to thank my wife, Lisa, for her love and encouragement as we continue our journey together.

Peter Hanfileti, MD

Vancouver, Washington

May, 2009

Terms of Use / Disclaimer

Information in this book is provided for informational purposes only and is not intended as a substitute for the advice provided by your physician or other healthcare professional. You should not use the information in this book for diagnosing or treating a health problem or disease, or prescribing any medication or other treatment.

This book is being sold with the understanding that the author is not engaged in rendering professional services. If professional advice or other expert assistance is required, the services of a competent professional person should be sought.

It is recommended that you consult with a healthcare professional for all of your child's medical needs *in person*. Do not rely on written, audio, video or other media sources only. This is in the best interest of you and your child. Ultimately, you must decide what is best for your child and family.

Table of Contents

The following Foreword to this book was written by Dr John Veltheim, the Founder of the BodyTalk System and someone who has influenced my career in countless ways over the past several years. I am deeply honored to have received his words of encouragement and grateful for his review of the manuscript of Energy Medicine Principles for Parents prior to its publication.

Peter Hanfileti, MD

Foreword

by Dr John Veltheim

Energy medicine has undergone very rapid development in the last ten years. Many recent scientific discoveries have shown much more about how the body really works, and have consequently brought the principles of energy medicine into the limelight.

One of the pivotal scientific discoveries made in recent times is one that supports the understanding long put forward in Traditional Chinese Medicine. Science has finally been able to establish that the old Cartesian model of treating the body, as if it were made up of many separately functioning parts, is wrong.

Scientific research now reveals that the human body is more like a hologram that runs as a result of complex energy field interactions. This revelation does not eschew the role of medical specialists but, instead, sheds light on the necessity for a new medical paradigm. In certain fields of medicine and specialization there are already signs that traditional doctors are looking for more answers in helping their patients. There are also significant numbers of patients looking into alternative ways of helping improve their own health.

Combine these shifts in perspective with the new, holistic, scientific model for treating the body and we find ourselves on the verge of a healthcare revolution. Books such as the one you are about to read are part and parcel of this healthcare revolution and evolution.

Dr Peter Hanfileti is one of those more enlightened Pediatricians who made the health of his patients his primary concern even if that meant exploring beyond the mainstream models of medicine. He has studied Acupuncture, which has a five thousand year tradition of great results, and, more recently, the BodyTalk System, which has a 14 year track record of results beyond the normal expectations of most health care practitioners. His studies confirmed that these systems do, in fact, have a very solid scientific basis behind them when examined with the insight of the new physics and biophysics promoted by such scientists as Dr James Oschman and Dr Bruce Lipton who have written prolifically on these subjects.

Dr Hanfileti keenly observes that these alternatives have offered very safe, and effective ways to address problems that the traditional medical model had no real answer for other than medication to relieve symptoms.

In Pediatrics, the BodyTalk System has proven to be of particular use in addressing the wide variety of childhood illnesses. The holistic principles of BodyTalk demonstrate that so many childhood disorders are environmentally caused or, at the very least, that the stress associated with environmental factors contributes greatly to the severity of the disease.

The BodyTalk model allows the practitioner insights into the dynamics of the family matrix and the many types of environmental stress that can be addressed by the system. This is particularly important with the many versions of mental emotional stress that can lead to learning and behavioral problems that are currently being suppressed by medication. Instead, alternative systems are proving that these problems can frequently be cured rather than controlled.

Further, BodyTalk puts heavy emphasis on understanding the enormous environmental impact on babies prenatally. Biophysics has shown that a baby will be affected by the stress of both parents and the lifestyle of the surrounding family matrix in the prenatal period. The BodyTalk System enables Dr Hanfileti to address these problems with pregnant mothers as well as in young children. A bonus is that the BodyTalk System requires no input of medication and is totally safe and non-invasive.

I have thoroughly enjoyed watching Peter grow into a leading practitioner of the BodyTalk System and I am impressed by the way he synthesizes this knowledge with his impressive medical background to have a groundbreaking Pediatric practice.

In the pages of this book you will enjoy his practical explanations of the approach he takes coupled with case studies that will change the way you think of health care forever.

Dr John Veltheim

Founder, The BodyTalk System
Sarasota, Florida
June, 2009

Introduction

This book is the result of my lifetime of experiences. Although most of what I am about to impart to you in this book has been developed and honed over the past 9 years in my clinical practice, it really started in my own childhood.

My first recollection of how the medical world impacted my life includes memories of getting immunizations as a child and then getting a lollipop from the doctor afterwards. I also recall getting my tonsils out around age 4 or 5 and calling the phlebotomist "stupid" after he poked my arm for the pre-op blood sample. Of course, I was rewarded with ice cream and 7-Up after the surgery which was quite a treat.

Perhaps the most important medical event for me occurred at about 7 years of age when I contracted meningitis while my family and I were living in Japan. I was hospitalized for 2 weeks and underwent multiple spinal taps, IV treatments and close observation. Meningitis affects the brain and spinal cord and causes symptoms like fever, seizures, achiness, blurry vision and weakness, all of which I experienced first hand.

It turned out that the causative organism was a virus and therefore no antibiotic could treat it. My parents recall how the Japanese doctor, who was a friend of our family, could not bear to stay in the room while I exhibited uncontrolled movements and cried in pain. Watchful waiting was all the doctors could do, and I recall my own parents' apprehension and worry about my status.

I distinctly remember hearing that some of the long term side effects of this condition could include things like hearing or vision loss, neurological impairment like chronic seizures or developmental delay, and even difficulty walking. That last one scared me so much I got up in the middle of the night while still in the hospital and I walked around the bed to prove to myself I could still use my legs.

Mind you, this happened in the context of my limited understanding and viewpoint as a seven year old. Nonetheless, it has stuck with me through all the intervening years as a poignant reminder of how a child's age and stage of maturation largely determines their responses to illnesses and events in their lives. I believe this experience for me helped to determine my path into the medical field and in particular into pediatrics.

Later in my middle school and high school years I was very interested in music and performed in various places playing the piano and oboe as well as singing in the school and church choirs. Music played a very important role in my formative years and I had many wonderful teachers and friends as examples to follow. Little did I know, that musical terms like harmony and resonance would come back to help me learn about energy medicine in my future. At the end of high school and then in college my focus and interest shifted to biology and science. I attended Earlham College and got my Bachelor's degree in biology. I was fascinated with the human body and its inner workings and I looked forward to learning more in medical school.

Medical School and Residency

I was fortunate to be accepted into the State University of New York at Buffalo Medical School where I spent 4 years learning and practicing to become a physician. One of my professors said something that has remained in my memory since then. He said, "It's better to have learned something once and then to have forgotten it, than to have never learned it at all." My interpretation of this is that it means you should be exposed to many sources of information, let them resonate with you for a time, and then move on to learn more. It's not about memorizing and knowing the right answers all the time, it's about being flexible and being able to interact with information and other people in a meaningful way, all the while taking into account the context and appropriateness of the information based on the scenario and circumstances.

After receiving my MD degree I was off to the University of Michigan for my 3 years of pediatric residency training. This included spending nights in one of the busiest hospitals in Michigan, *C.S. Mott Children's Hospital*, and taking care of some of the sickest babies and children. It was quite a whirlwind of intellectual stimulation, stress, sleep deprivation, close camaraderie, privileged interaction with family and colleagues, and a proving ground for being able to make it out in the real world of everyday medicine.

Life and Death

One of the things I loved best about working with children while in my residency was witnessing their incredible ability to get better in almost all instances. I was thankful to participate in the triumphs and joys of recovery with these kids and their families. But not every child recovered from their illness and I remember those children and their families vividly. Although it was difficult, I am honored to have experienced the grief and witnessed the love of parents and families going through loss and tragedy.

The memory of one particular young man with cancer still echoes in my mind. I recall his pleas for help to stop his pain. I remember feeling helpless and at a loss for what to do. From a medical standpoint he was already taking the maximum doses of the medication we could provide.

This is where one's humanity is really put to the test. When there are no answers and little in the way of words to provide comfort we must provide good old fashioned hand holding and empathy. It is by far the most difficult position for a physician to be in but it is also a reminder that the broad range of experiences we witness benefits us all, whether we are the ones going through it or whether we are simply the observer/helper.

Another event that stopped me in my tracks was the untimely and shocking death of one of my fellow pediatric residents who was killed in a car accident. These events have no explanation or reason, and I recall having to lead my team on the hospital wards the very next morning to take care of the patients we were responsible for. This was a strong reminder of the ephemeral nature of life itself and a quick course correction for those of us who might have become complacent or stuck in the daily grind of routines and mundane pursuits.

After completing my pediatric residency my wife, Lisa, and I moved to the Pacific Northwest and settled in Vancouver, Washington where we live currently. I happily joined a pediatric group practice and assumed I would work for 30-40 years and then retire after a rewarding career. I did practice for about 6 years as a general pediatrician, handling everything from newborns in the hospital to well child checkups, sick visits, sutures for lacerations and cuts, and spending time with parents trying to give them the best advice I could.

My Introduction to Acupuncture

This might have been the end of the story of my experience in the medical world, if it had not been for my gradual and progressive exposure and interest in the alternative medicine paradigm. This came about when my wife, Lisa, tried acupuncture for headaches and insomnia and got good results. She then decided to go to school to become an acupuncturist. I was skeptical to say the least, and I remember thinking and asking, "If this stuff really works, where is the research and why was I never taught this in medical school?" It is only now in retrospect that I can see how that way of thinking has been an impediment to the mindset of physicians for too long. When I started to learn more about the Chinese medicine system and the nature of its philosophy and how logical and all-encompassing it is, my life was changed forever.

I personally tried acupuncture and took some Chinese herbs prescribed by one of my wife's professors in the late 1990's. My own body's response included a decrease in blood pressure, weight loss, and feeling relaxed and less stressed in my work. I began my own studies of the subject of Chinese medicine and eventually I became certified and started using acupuncture with my own patients, mostly teenagers with sports injuries. These kids in my own practice responded so quickly to acupuncture that I knew I had to explore this further and take it as far as I could. Within a couple of years it became apparent that I would have to choose between continuing my conventional practice as a pediatrician, or branching out on my own to practice in the style I believed was most beneficial to the children and parents I had taken an oath to treat. I made the decision to leave my group practice in June of 2000 and my wife and I opened the clinic we currently have today.

What I now call energy medicine is a combination of several different medical systems that embrace the simple notion that we as human beings are much more than our anatomy and physiology reveals. What I learned in my conventional medical training was no doubt useful and necessary, but I did not realize how incomplete it was until I became exposed to these energy based concepts. Seeing kids in my practice over the last several years has taught me even more about the energy dynamics that play a role in all aspects of health and well being for kids and families.

How to Use this Book

I want to share these insights with you because I know they can be extremely helpful to you as you navigate through the growing years with your child. Since every child is different, you as the parent will have to decide if this information and way of looking at your family's situation is right for you. I encourage you to read through this material with an open mind, and take in what feels right to you and keep on the back burner any thing else.

This book is divided into 4 main sections. In Part I, I have listed 10 energy medicine principles I think all parents should know about. In Part II, the BodyTalk System is introduced and described, knowing that one must actually experience a treatment to fully understand what it's all about. In Part III we delve into pediatric applications and the importance of your child's age and stage of development and how this impacts their energy medicine evaluation and treatment. In Part IV, called energy medicine synthesis, I will give you 3 real case studies from my own practice to show you how we put all of this information together as a coherent plan of action as part of your child's energy medicine evaluation.

If you are inclined to jump to a specific section of this book, go right ahead and do so. However, I recommend that you read through the whole thing and refer back to certain sections when necessary to refresh your memory. This is an ongoing process and I hope it will continue to evolve and grow as your child matures and develops over the years.

It has taken me several years to feel comfortable with the shedding of my old skin as a conventional pediatrician. Even today, I still see physicians rolling their eyes (just the way I did) when I discuss energy medicine concepts. It has always been the parents (whose children have benefitted greatly from this approach) who have supported and encouraged me to get this information into the hands of as many people who will listen.

I used to think that meant sharing my knowledge one-on-one with parents in the treatment room. But with the power of the Internet I now have the ability to communicate to a global community of concerned parents who are looking for help for their children.

So even if you are a parent I might never meet, I want to thank you for taking the initiative to learn about energy medicine. I believe it is a huge piece that is missing from our current understanding of health and illness today. More importantly, energy medicine provides the most effective form of treatment I know of for children. And it does not have the costly (both physically and financially) side effects and limitations that conventional medical treatments often involve.

My unique life experiences, training, and knowledge provide a perspective on your child's energy system that I know can help you understand your child better. I always tell parents that your time with your child while they are growing up is precious and limited. So make good use of the time you have, learn all you can, and use this book as a springboard to propel you toward other books, videos, and resources to educate yourself and to help your child reach their greatest potential. I wish you and your child the very best on your journey together.

Part I: Energy Medicine Principles

We shall not cease from exploration,
and the end of all our exploring will be
to arrive where we started
and know the place for the first time.

T.S. Eliot

In the first part of this book I will explain ten energy medicine principles that I believe all parents should know about. These ten principles will lay the foundation for your understanding of energy medicine and how these concepts relate to your individual child.

I have chosen these ten specific principles because they come up most often in the conversations that I have with parents. I have tried to write using the same terminology that I use every day with parents in my clinical practice. Because this information is most likely new to you, I have included many examples to help illustrate these energy medicine principles. So even if you do not initially understand everything I write, please continue reading and I am sure it will become clear.

Energy Medicine Principle #1: Distribution

The first principle is called Distribution. Your child has what I call individual "settings" which determine how their energy is distributed throughout their system. These settings are put into place by your child's system based on the historical events they have experienced combined with the current environmental influences and triggers they are exposed to.

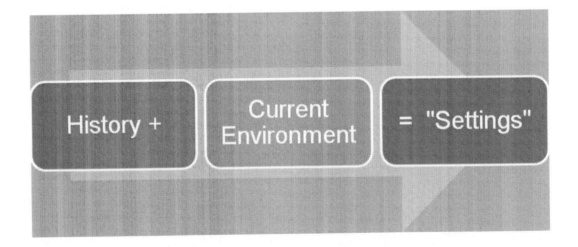

Let me explain. Your child's nervous system (brain) functions with the underlying notion that what has come before (history) in their experience may come again. This makes complete sense when you think about how our lives play out chronologically and how we learn over time. This aspect is added to the inputs which come from our experience of our current

surroundings in both physical and non-physical forms.

Another way to explain this is to relate how you probably have "settings"

that you use in your workplace in accordance with your job title and

different "settings" that you use at home as mother or father. This idea of

using different energy settings for different situations is something we all do

automatically.

In the energy medicine system of your child it works the same way. Your

child will have settings for day and night, school and home, weekdays and

weekends. I will use this term called "settings" throughout this book so I

want you to be clear about what I am referring to.

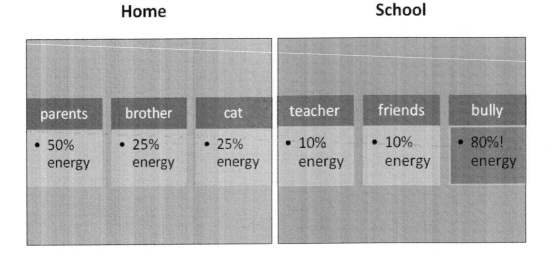

"Settings"
An example of a child's home vs. school settings by percentage energy expenditure

Home			School		
parents	brother	cat	teacher	friends	bully
• 50% energy	• 25% energy	• 25% energy	• 10% energy	• 10% energy	• 80%! energy

In this figure you can see an example of how a child's energy system might use different settings at home versus in school and how their energy expenditure is skewed towards the stress of dealing with a bully while at school. My point is that the extra effort and energy needed to deal with a bully in school contrasts sharply with their settings at home. This is an example of how your child's energy settings can vary in different situations. One of the fascinating things about this concept of settings is that they are different for each person, even for those within the same family. If you

28

have more than one child you will know what I'm talking about. Even

identical twins, although very similar, will have different settings and

individual characteristics that set them apart from each other.

Some kids are high energy and on the go, while other kids are more laid

back and mellow most of the time. Some children have settings that cause

an interest in more physical activity as an outlet, others prefer to read and

engage in more intellectual pursuits. In addition, I often see kids whose

settings are set to avoid a particular situation or feeling.

A child's settings can be reinforced or triggered by both internal and

external events. For example, if you were bitten by a dog when you were a

child, you may have a fear of dogs and this might be triggered by seeing a

dog, even if it's on a leash and not a threat. This visual cue can result in

activating the setting that is stored in your system which says, "Oh no!

That dog might bite me! I had better be very careful around this dog." This

makes logical sense based on your earlier experience.

| I'm scared of dogs! |

| I love playing with dogs! |

Someone else who did not experience being bitten by a dog like you did, might go running toward a dog in their vicinity and want to reach out and pet him. Do you see the difference in settings here? All of us have settings like these that operate automatically and often they are hidden below our level of awareness.

One of the keys to understanding how your child's energy system functions is to become aware of these motivating forces that may be playing a role in your child's daily energy distribution settings. Keep this in mind as you learn and reflect on what your child's history and life experiences have been so far. This principle of distribution is one I use on a daily basis to describe what's happening with my patients and their energy settings.

Energy Medicine Principle #2: Hierarchy

The simplest way to relate the principle of hierarchy is to borrow the concept of an "ordered list" from the Chinese medicine system. Chinese medicine has been used as an effective form of health care for thousands of years, and can be used today along side modern medicine mostly in the form of acupuncture and herbal therapies.

Chinese medicine describes the flow of energy in the body through pathways called channels or meridians. These channels are further categorized into sub-systems which include its associated organ along with multiple functions and correspondences. While I will not go into a full description of the Chinese medicine system because it is beyond the scope of this book, I will give an example of how we can use this very elegant system to help us understand your child.

One of the 12 primary subsystems is the Liver organ and meridian circuit. We use the term circuit because this denotes the energy characteristic of this system rather than just the physical organ concept that we are most familiar with from a conventional medical point of view.

The liver organ functions as a detoxification organ and the liver meridian runs from the big toe (both left and right sides) all the way up the front of the legs and abdomen to the front of the ribs in the chest area.

Liver energy sub-circuit

voluntary muscles and movement, eyes, menstrual periods, stresses, anger, frustration, preparation, organization

In addition, the liver as a subsystem is responsible for the energy distribution required for such things as normal voluntary muscle movement, health of the eyes, menstrual periods, dealing with environmental and other internal and external stresses, the emotions of anger and frustration, and the cognitive function of preparing and organizing ones' thoughts.

These are all correlated by your child's energy system automatically and preferentially taken care of in order of priority. It turns out that for this particular circuit, the job of dealing with stressors takes priority over many of the other functions that the liver has to manage. It is not surprising, then, when a child experiences a stress-provoking event in their lives, many times symptoms will crop up in one or more of these other areas that the liver is supposed to take care of.

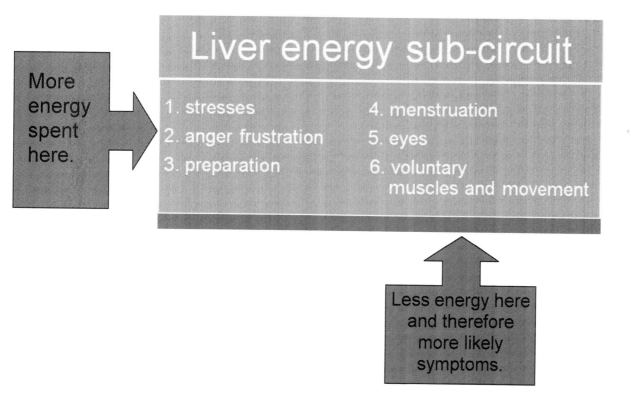

I have found this principle of hierarchy combined with the Chinese medicine channel and organ correspondences to be one of the most useful ways to evaluate a child's state. It often provides the necessary framework to explain mysterious conditions or behaviors that up until then have seemed to occur for no apparent reason. In the above example, if we can identify the stressors which are taking up a lot of energy in a child's liver energy system, this can lead to strategies to rebalance and return the system to more normal function.

If we are not aware of these correspondences, then we will mistakenly focus only on the symptom and miss the underlying root cause or trigger that the child's system is trying to compensate for. I highly recommend that you educate yourself on this topic of Chinese medicine or find a practitioner that can help your child benefit from this effective energy medicine system.

In my practice I am continually using this principle of hierarchy in my conversations with patients and parents as well as in my own mind as I formulate treatment strategies. Using this hierarchy principle of energy priority is also valuable to you as the parent because it can give you a greater understanding of what is going on with your child.

Energy Medicine Principle #3: Conservation

Conservation is a term I use to depict what your child's energy system does to maintain and protect itself. As I mentioned earlier, your child experiences the world as a series of events in chronologic order from their prenatal and birth experience up to the present time.

It has been my experience that those events which are most significant in your child's life will have what I call "savings accounts" associated with them. These are energy reservoirs for that "just in case" scenario. What I mean is this; if your child has experienced something they perceived as traumatic or threatening, their system will automatically set up a savings account of energy just in case that same event happens again.

Saving energy "just in case"

This is something we all do naturally throughout our lives. But as young children we tend to overreact and expend extraordinary amounts of energy when we don't have a mature context in which to place our experiences.

An example might be having surgery like getting your tonsils removed. As a child it is easy to live through this and have the mistaken notion that this exact procedure might need to be repeated again and again. As adults we know this is not the case, but as a 4 or 5 year old, you can see where this mistaken impression could arise and result in the storing up of energy to be prepared just in case it happens again.

I'd better be ready for this next time it happens!

Another important facet of the principle of conservation is the idea that while the settings are appropriate in the short term, over the long term and with continued life experiences, these settings outlive their usefulness and need to be "updated" to reflect your child's current level of function and maturity.

This should ideally include energy expenditures which are in keeping with your child's current needs and which are optimized according to their current stage of development. For example, a teenager whose system is (unconsciously) expending energy on the notion that they may need their tonsils removed again, would be wasting energy unnecessarily. They would be better served by redistributing and rebalancing their energy system to match their current state.

Use the principle of conservation to understand more of how your child's energy system functions and how events as "normal" as a tonsillectomy can leave a lasting effect.

Energy Medicine Principle #4: Imprinting

One thing I have found to be extremely important is the age your child was at the time their current settings were first put in place. This energy medicine principle is called imprinting. What happens is that the association of inputs coming from your child's five senses along with their internal stage of development is joined together in a setting that persists over time.

If we expand further on the previously mentioned scenario of a child having their tonsils out, the nervous system's tendency to make associations deserves further discussion here. I have seen cases where associations are made with the hospital environment, the doctor's office, the time of year, the smell of sterilizing solution and many other types of triggers that cause a reinforcing phenomenon and further energy expenditure of the child's system. And all of these energetic associations (which can lead to very real physical conditions) stem from their original experience of having their tonsils out.

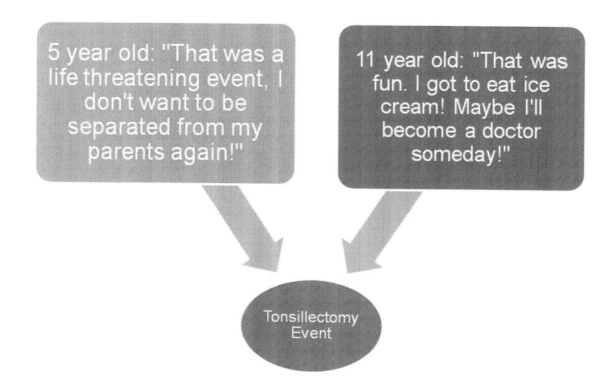

In addition, the child's stage of development at the time plays an important role in how the event is interpreted and catalogued. In the figure above you can see where a young child's system might store the memory of having their tonsils out and being separated from their parents for a short time in the hospital as "a life threatening event" versus an older child who might recall the same episode as a fun excursion away from home where they were offered ice cream in bed!

These age-related differences are very important and ones I frequently look for and point out to parents in my practice. See if you can pinpoint how and when your child's settings were originally put in place. This will give you tremendous insight into what is driving those underlying motivations and

the all important energy expenditures and distribution patterns in your

child's system.

Energy Medicine Principle #5: Resonance

"A bird doesn't sing because it has an answer,
it sings because it has a song."

-Maya Angelou

The next principle is called resonance. In musical terms the same

frequency or note played at the same time results in sympathetic

resonance. If a guitar or violin string is plucked and there is another

stringed instrument nearby with the same resonant frequency, that string

will begin to vibrate as well.

This concept leads us to the Neurolinguistic Programming (NLP) technique

of getting in rapport (in synchrony) with your child. Another way to describe this is getting in rhythm with your child's natural flow of energy. As I have mentioned, the energy distribution of your child is very individual and it is very useful for you to know this about them. Furthermore, this energy pattern changes over time and even minute to minute. Getting in rapport with your child means matching the state they are in and either staying there with them, or helping them to move on to another state of being.

For example, let's say it is getting near the time to go to school. If your child is still in bed, you can get in rapport with them by slowly moving about in their room, talking quietly to them and then progressively you may get louder and more animated over several minutes. In this way, you will lead them into a more awake state and help them to get moving.

 Another example might be getting in rapport with your child when they are feeling bored. You can empathize with their current state of boredom and then gently suggest an activity or brainstorming to find something to do.

In this way, you can lead them out of their state of feeling bored and into a more exciting activity. It is even better if it appears that the new activity was all their idea! This principle of resonance has far reaching implications throughout your child's growth and development years.

I want to introduce another concept that fits in here which I call, "age reciprocal resonance". One of the many fascinating observations that I have made in my experience with treating both children and parents is the existence of energy that flows in terms of a two way street (between parents and their kids). This is not that surprising when you think about how closely we resemble our parents and take on many of their characteristics as our own.

What I was not prepared for was the idea of "age reciprocal resonance" which sets up a scenario where your child is stimulating their own age counterpart in you, and you are stimulating your child to respond to that younger part of you. Let's look at the following hypothetical example.

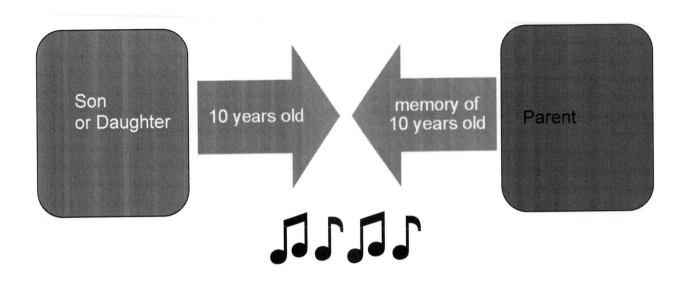

Your child is like a walking neon sign that continuously says, "This is what it means to be 10 years old". From an energy perspective, this is a very powerful influence and one you as the parent cannot turn off or ignore. What happens automatically is your own memory of your experience as a 10 year old comes to the forefront within your own energy system.

Now what happens is that your child has access to *your* experience as a 10 year old because it is now prominent in your energy field. I have seen cases where the child is actually expending energy trying to "solve" the issue being broadcast by the parent's younger self.

This, of course, is not a desirable situation and no parent would choose to borrow their own child's energy system for this purpose. However, if this remains unconscious, it will work behind the scenes and cause friction or at the very least some imbalances either in the relationship between the parent and child or internally within the child's system itself.

I feel this topic is very important for all parents to know about, especially if they have a child who is more on the sensitive side and who may be more prone to this phenomenon. The proactive step you can take as a parent is to investigate and work on your own childhood issues well before your child reaches those age ranges where they may have age reciprocal resonance implications with you. I will revisit this topic later on when we discuss the family matrix, so stay tuned.

Energy Medicine Principle #6: Harmony

Next is the principle of harmony. This principle is about different frequencies existing in a complementary fashion. Remember, when we are talking about your child's energy system, it is very individual to them, and yet they must fit into your overall family structure.

If you have more than one child, they will each gravitate towards opposite ends of the spectrum, sometimes very early in their development. Often this is best handled when complementary opposites are allowed to coexist, but not to any extremes.

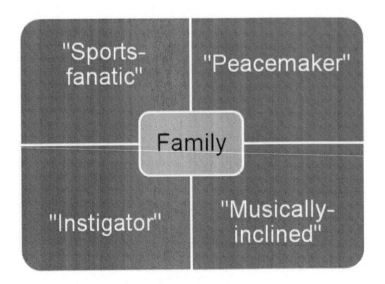

For example, one child may take on the role of peacemaker, the other the role of instigator. There is nothing wrong with this, as long as there is not pressure to stay in this role forever, or to conform to it for external reasons.

Another example might be one child who is interested in music, while the other is interested in sports. There must be a balance between choosing roles and activities just to be distinct from the other sibling(s), and doing those activities because that child has a true desire to pursue those interests.

Thus, harmony should be strived for both within the family unit and internally within the child, in accordance with their true underlying blueprint, which only they can know.

It is also important to emphasize and demonstrate that they have the freedom to change their settings at any time. In other words, they should not feel locked into a certain pattern just because it has been that way for a long time.

The analogy would be a song that maintains the same harmonic structure throughout the entire piece; this would be boring indeed. It is a good thing to try and find the harmonic chord settings and changes that are most appropriate for your child.

If we take this musical analogy one step further, I think it can be said that the opposite of harmony, which is dissonance or tension, can be used as an opportunity to seek resolution and thus enhance the function of learning. It is my opinion that this cycle must repeat itself over and over again for your child to truly "get it". Only after many instances and experiences will your child make the connection that change is good and necessary for their own growth, development, and lifelong progression.

Giving your child the freedom to move and change among many different settings within the family unit as well as individually will lead to a more balanced outcome. This is the essence of the principle of harmony.

Energy Medicine Principle #7: Time Independence

Being independent of time constraints is what this next principle is about.

From an energy perspective, the passage of time has little bearing or

influence on those settings which are put in place for compelling and

sometimes emergent reasons. In fact, this leads to the notion that the

longer a setting has been in existence, the stronger your child's energy

system will work to keep it that way.

In my current practice I see patients of all age groups including adults, and

what I have found is that even those settings that were put in place years

49

ago during childhood can have an ongoing energy influence in an older person.

This reliance on "default settings" is a paradox when compared to the constantly changing environment we live in. I can only explain this by saying it seems to be dependent on the impact of the initiating event and the person's age at the time.

For example, a scary event like a car accident can still have an energy influence on a person decades later which takes the form of anxiety or nervousness whenever they are in a moving car. Often the person will not make this correlation until we bring it out during the history taking interview. From an energy perspective, it does not matter how much time has elapsed since the event. The important fact is that it is still influencing the person's energy system dynamics and distribution.

When it comes to your child's situation, I want you to think about the events they may have experienced already that could have this type of far reaching, time-independent influence. Some of the more common types of events I see in my practice are, death of a grandparent, change of school, moving to a new house, loss of a pet, and parental divorce.

When you have the knowledge and the means to address these energetic imbalances you can treat them before your child incorporates the event as part of their daily energy expenditures. This preventative approach is one of the tremendous advantages of undergoing an energy medicine evaluation and treatment.

Of course, intervening sooner rather than later can save you and your child a lot of time and effort in the long run. I encourage you to explore this area thoroughly with your child and family because the benefits of prevention are well worth it.

Energy Medicine Principle #8: Space Independence

This next principle refers to energy and its independence from space limitations. Energy is not limited to physical structures. In the same way that sunlight can travel across space and cause a farmer's crops to grow on Earth, energy can travel at tremendous speed and result in simultaneous experience.

What I am about to say is another example of a clinical observation that I never would have thought possible prior to my exploration of the energy medicine paradigm.

Your energy connection to your child is not dependent on your location. You can be at work and you will still have a direct energetic influence on your child while they are in school.

Even after kids grow up and move out of the house, I have seen instances where a parent-child duo can have significant experiences happening at the same time even though they are separated by quite a distance. How can we explain this? The energy medicine system allows for this to be explained by this principle of space independence.

53

In physics the term they use is non-locality. According to Mark Comings, a physicist and lecturer, even the void out in deep space which used to be considered empty, is now confirmed to contain enormous amounts of energy. In addition, experiments have been done which show that atomic particles separated by great distances can respond to changes in the other particle in an instant, showing that energy connections exist that we barely can explain. I don't think it's that much of a stretch to think this can happen in the real world between two people who are just made up of energy particles themselves.

Getting back to you and your child, just keep in mind that your energy connection with your child is continuous and has an impact on them. I often recommend that parents send or broadcast thoughts and feelings to their kids in addition to giving them verbal statements. This can reassure your youngster if they are picking up stressful signals or other energy inputs coming from you without you being aware that this is happening.

This energy connection is a two way street, and you could very well be picking up on your child's energy changes throughout the day while they are away at school and vice versa. If your child is extra sensitive, ask them if they feel differences throughout the day when they are away from home and see what kind of responses you get.

Even when babies and toddlers are preverbal, they will exhibit changes even when you go to a different part of the house or answer the phone. Just remember that this principle of space independence of your child's energy system is active and can explain many instances of coincidental experiences between the two of you.

Even previous generational influences or inherited predispositions can be explained in these energy terms but we will leave that discussion to another time.

Energy Medicine Principle #9: Ubiquity

Energy is omnipresent. No matter where you look, energy is present in some form. This contrasts with the "5 senses only" view we are used to. We have a tendency to view the world as finite and only accessible through our five senses.

But if everything has energy associated with it, we must conclude that your child's energy system is connected to the whole universe. I believe that the degree of sensitivity of your child is directly proportional to this connection. I have seen kids who are so sensitive they can be affected by things happening to other kids in their classroom or school.

And there are some super-sensitive kids who can be affected by what's happening in distant places in the world. Of course, the internet and television give kids immediate access to this information along with striking images, but the fact remains that some kids are much more prone to experience these external events in a personal way that affects their own energy field.

Another example I have seen is where a location like a public place or building carries an energy association which can be picked up by a sensitive child.

Often there is no historical information available, but the child will feel the sensation or emotional component that relates to some previous event that happened there. I know this sounds farfetched but to the child and the family that have experienced this, it is very real, and certainly deserves an explanation if the pieces of the puzzle can be discerned.

My observation is that this degree of heightened sensitivity has become

more common in recent years, especially among the kids I see in my

clinical practice. The principle of energy ubiquity means that there are

energy correlations and associations all around us. It can have a significant

impact on a child's energy system and should not be overlooked.

Energy Medicine Principle #10: Intelligence

"The true sign of intelligence is not knowledge but imagination."

-Albert Einstein

Energy systems, like your child's nervous system, operate with an intelligence that seeks to learn, understand, and then it moves on to the next level. Another way to describe this is that your child's development leads to learning new lessons, which in turn leads to the constant seeking of new opportunities to meet their potential.

To borrow a phrase from Star Trek, the "prime directive" for your child is to "go where no one has gone before" and this means your child's underlying directive is to become an individual and to become independent. Your child's system is designed to see and evaluate contrast, and to move toward the best choice in the most efficient and intelligent manner possible.

In this way, change is constantly occurring in your child's experience and it can be hard for them to keep up with the pace. You can play an important role in helping your child to move through these stages in a smooth and coherent manner. You can also promote the natural occurrence of these gains and changes according to your child's individual time frame, not conforming to some readymade standard or set schedule.

I believe in the intelligence of your child's underlying energy system. Your child's body and system knows what to do. In many cases, we just have to get out of the way and allow the natural process to take its course. I will expand on this topic of systemic intelligence later in our discussion of The BodyTalk System.

Finally, one last comment I want to make about these ten energy medicine principles, is that your child's very living consciousness, one of the highest forms of energy there is, utilizes all of these principles all the time. I want you to think about this for a minute and just recognize the implications of this statement.

These principles are ongoing in real time, not fixed in the past as historical precedents. In addition, since these are energy related parameters, they are not going to be obvious to you or your child. You must look for them

and nurture their development if you want your child to make progress in

the most harmonious and balanced way they can.

Part II: The Treatment Process and The BodyTalk System

**"The intuitive mind is a sacred gift
and the rational mind is a faithful servant.
We have created a society that honors the servant
and has forgotten the gift."**

−Albert Einstein

In this next section, I will discuss the logistics of how I treat kids and in particular how I use The BodyTalk System as one of the primary modalities in my practice.

After a brief description of how I discovered this accurate and effective method of assessment and treatment, I will relate my understanding of the theory at work when we participate in BodyTalk treatments. I will also give you the 'nuts and bolts' of how I conduct sessions in my practice.

Many of the phrases I use in this section are taken right out of the common descriptions I give to kids and their parents in my office. I am grateful to all of those families I have interacted with, for they have contributed to my ongoing learning and understanding of this dynamic and changing field.

63

The BodyTalk System

I was introduced to BodyTalk in a most mysterious way. I received a letter in the mail from someone I had never met, informing me that a speaker was coming whom I had never heard of, and he was to discuss a kinesiology-based bodywork technique that I had never imagined could become part of my repertoire as a physician practicing in the United States.

This curious twist of fate happened right when I was in the middle of transitioning from a conventional pediatrics group practice to the alternative medicine based practice I have today. I had always wanted to treat kids with non-invasive approaches whenever possible, and in my opinion, BodyTalk is the ultimate system when it comes to natural, gentle, respectful techniques used in the treatment of children.

I must admit that it took a lot of convincing and practice before I was able to shake loose from my previously indoctrinated western physician mind-set. The rewards for my persistence have been well worth it, however, as I now am able to practice and learn the most interesting things from my youngest patients on a daily basis.

This new field of study for me has followed the same pattern which was started when I began my studies of the Chinese medicine system. Learning about energy medicine for me has been like being in a continuously enlarging field. Since the process started I have been in a never-ending progression of gaining more knowledge and clinical experience.

Starting from my conventional medical training and practice as a general primary care pediatrician, and then winding through the world of alternative medicine, it has been a long and meandering pathway indeed. Much of my more recent insight into the pediatric age group comes from using The BodyTalk System, which I will explain in more detail shortly.

If you are a parent with one or more children, you are probably always looking for ways to better treat or at least understand what is going on with your youngster. As a trained pediatrician with many years of experience, I can say without a doubt that the best healthcare approach for your child is the one that encompasses the most territory and the one that is most open to the *individual* nature of your child. I realize this is quite a broad and sweeping statement, but I firmly believe that it is true.

The way that most conventionally trained physicians are taught leaves out the majority of what I believe are the most important causative factors in a child's development and wellbeing. These factors are largely unseen and remain dormant to those that are unaware of their existence. I hope this book will shed some light on the multidimensional aspects of how we are affected by the energy dynamics occurring all around us both currently and historically.

Energy medicine is the term that used to describe the future of medicine but now that future is here in the present. In this age of super information and the internet, the boundaries that used to divide different schools of thought and fields of study have now become obsolete. What this means is previously separated subjects have come together to produce overlapping understandings and this includes the fields of medicine, mathematics, music, physics, and all the rest. Countless authors from many diverse backgrounds have written about the same truths over and over again. I think it's about time we put these facts together in a consistent cohesive manner that makes logical sense and let go of the need to conserve outdated modes of thinking.

BodyTalk as a system brings together these many different systems and treats them as equally important and potentially beneficial to the individual, if presented in the right order and with the right quality and clarity of communication.

BodyTalk Theory

> *"The BodyTalk System is a unique healthcare modality in that it addresses the body in a truly integrative, holistic way. The BodyTalk practitioner recognizes that the body mind complex functions as a synchronicity, and not as a bundle of autonomously functioning parts...*
>
> *Also, by means of biofeedback, the body's innate wisdom indicates its priorities in bringing about enhanced communication within the body mind complex.*
>
> *The act of tapping on the head enables innate to register these links in the brain, which enhances the overall integral functioning and intercommunication within the body. The act of tapping over the heart complex enables innate to store the memory of these links. In this way, the innate wisdom and healing function inherent in the body is enhanced on all levels-physical, mental, emotional and spiritual."*
>
> Excerpt from *The BodyTalk System* by John Veltheim,
> Module 1, 3rd Edition, 2002

I am indebted to Dr John Veltheim and Esther Veltheim, who have partnered over the years to bring the concepts and practical uses of The BodyTalk System to the U.S. and the rest of the world. The BodyTalk training program consists of a series of modules and seminars. It is practiced by trained professionals and laypeople alike. If you are interested you may find out more about this fascinating modality on the International BodyTalk Association website at http://www.bodytalksystem.com.

Parents often ask me, "What's actually happening in the process of giving and receiving a BodyTalk treatment?" It is not an easy question to answer because although the BodyTalk process *looks* very simplistic, there is actually A LOT going on! Technically speaking, the BodyTalk process works through a combination of mechanisms and interactions. These interactions are both between the client and practitioner, and within each individual. By combining the kinesiology response, the practitioner based left-brain navigation through the BodyTalk protocol, and the intuitive openness of the right-brain function, information is accessed which focuses the client's attention on a particular 'category' that needs balancing.

The practitioner taps the head and chest while the patient is relaxed and breathing easily. Then the next category is found and addressed. A third person or the parent themselves is often able to detect and feel the energy treatment taking place, even though the tapping is not taking place on them directly.

I can say that as a practitioner, my own experience while doing BodyTalk treatments is quite variable and all across the spectrum. Sometimes I feel calm and peaceful along with the patient, other times I may feel energy movement within my own body or I may see images or get certain impressions internally that may or may not have significance for the patient.

The importance of energy as a mode of communication and treatment is as follows:

1) Human beings (as well as inanimate things) produce and emit energy, which in turn moves and has effects on other living beings and non-living things.

2) Energy moves in at least two simultaneous directions.

These simple statements fill a huge gap when it comes to our currently

accepted medical view and I am delighted to say that when most parents

grasp the meaning of this they finally understand how complex the

variables are that affect their child on a daily basis.

The BodyTalk Treatment

When it comes to the actual treatment of pediatric patients, I take a fairly

flexible approach based on the child's age and comfort level. Obviously,

parents are included in the history taking and treatment and they will often

know whether or not the child will tolerate hands on treatment.

The child can sit or lie down with or without the parent beside them. Some

older kids may prefer to be alone for the treatment and that is their

prerogative. For younger kids and prenatal treatments we simply use the

mother to access the child's energy system which is strongly linked to her.

The kinesiology portion of The BodyTalk System is an ingenious balance of

left-brain dependent category navigation and right-brained intuitive exploration. My role as a practitioner is to methodically go through the body mind categories, while trying to tune in to the child's systemic needs based on their own innate "priority list". The result is that usually several links come up as being beneficial to tap out and this signals the child's system (autonomic nervous system or autopilot) to begin the process of balancing, communicating, and synchronizing itself.

This process emphasizes specific imbalances so the child's system can address them. In this way, information can be brought to the collective awareness of the child, the parents, and the practitioner. And since energy has effects which travel in both directions (to and from), changes can be encouraged to take place for the betterment of the child's overall condition.

Part III: Pediatric Applications

There is always one moment in childhood
when the door opens and lets the future in.

-Deepak Chopra

I'm going to divide this section on pediatric applications by age group, because there are vast differences between them. First we'll talk about treating pregnant mothers in the prenatal stage and then move on to babies, toddlers, school age, and teenagers. One of the advantages of being in pediatrics is that the tremendous variety we see tends to be easily categorized by age. This is further enhanced by the developmental gains made by children in relatively short periods of time. I believe this lends itself to many of the techniques that work well in managing common childhood issues. (Please read my "8 Tips for Parents". It is available for free download in both video and ebook formats on my website at www.principlesforparents.com)

Prenatal

I have had the privilege of treating mothers at various stages of their pregnancies. This is a very special experience and one which offers tremendous advantages when it comes to prevention and getting the baby off to a great start in life.

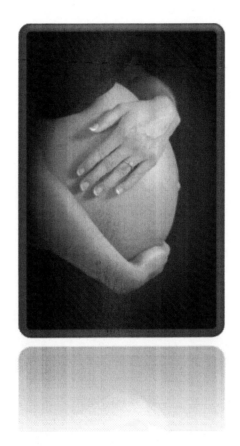

One undeniable fact I have learned through BodyTalk, is that babies are exposed to all aspects of the mother's experience during and well after the pregnancy period. The energy medicine paradigm allows us to put into

perspective the different energy influences that the baby experiences.

For example, if a pregnant mother slips and falls on the stairs, there is a

natural immediate fear about her baby's wellbeing. When she gets

checked over by her obstetrician and is reassured that everything is fine,

this should be the end of the story. But the question we must ask is, "How

does this experience register in the baby's body, mind, and nervous

system?" I call these episodes "imprints" because they can have a long

lasting effect on what the baby considers a 'priority', and therefore

something they will expend energy on.

Now the timing of this event is crucial, because it predates the birth

experience. In essence, this episode becomes part of this baby's

"introduction to the world". The baby's energy system may interpret the

meaning of this event as, "My security can be threatened whenever mom is

on the stairs." You can see how this imprint can become reinforced every

time the mother goes up or down the stairs. This imprinting process affects

the baby through the mother's experiences, both internally with her feelings and thoughts, and externally with her outward life experiences during the pregnancy.

It has also been my experience that all of these prenatal influences will have a tendency to be ongoing and very strong throughout the child's early years and beyond if they are not dealt with in a clear and proactive manner. It is certainly true that intervening sooner rather than later is much easier when it comes to energy medicine as an influence. This is why focusing on treating young children, babies, and the mother in the prenatal period is so important.

Birth

The birth event for a child is a milestone like no other. The impact of the

first few minutes, hours, and days becomes the experiential introduction to

the world for them.

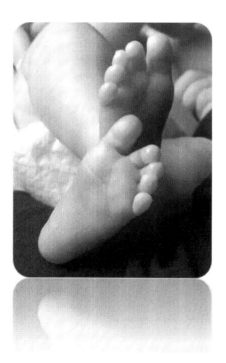

Three important factors I would like parents to recognize are:

1) The baby's energy system, including the brain, which serves as their five senses recording device, is fully functional although immature.

2) They operate from day one assuming that all that happens in their experience is normal and will continue in perpetuity.

3) The two way energy exchange between parents, siblings, and the baby is in full force and influences everything that all members of the family experience.

Let's look at each one of these factors individually.

Our five senses are the filters through which we experience the world. You may already know that hearing is functioning in a developing baby at 20 weeks gestational age. From then on, all sounds the baby is exposed to (like the parents' voices) are registered and categorized by the growing infant's brain. Studies have shown that a newborn will turn toward the sound of the mother's or father's voice right after birth. This demonstrates that they have the ability to distinguish sounds as "safe" and they are hardwired to want to be in close proximity to familiar energy sources.

What I would like to point out is that hearing and the other four senses are just one facet of how the newborn takes in information about the surrounding world. Here again, the energy medicine paradigm allows us to understand and interpret certain behaviors that a newborn exhibits with more clarity than we may have previously thought possible.

Consider the scenario when the mother is on the phone and the baby starts to cry. The mother is still physically nearby, the baby hears her voice, and yet something causes the reaction of crying in the infant. What could be going on? If we allow for the notion that the baby is detecting a moderate diverting of the mother's attention and this is interpreted by the immature brain as "threatening" to the energetic bond the baby has with the mother, this reaction becomes readily understandable.

BodyTalk is able to address this purely energy related response and help the infant's system prioritize and balance the influence as part of the learning process and not as something unusual that needs to be feared.

Moving on to the second point, babies operate with the programming that says "what's happening is normal and will continue forever". This is a result of how the immature brain works.

The birth process itself is a transformation from intrauterine life in water, to extra uterine life in air and the rest of the three dimensional world. For some babies, this is a tough transition to fully process and may take months to years to reconcile internally. This is the type of scenario where exposing the baby to small changes and then reinforcing the fact that these changes (like the mother being in another room for 15 seconds) can be tolerated and lived through serves as "practice" for the developing nervous system. Eventually, the baby's operating program that takes over says "I can handle small changes for short periods of time, learn from them, and still know that certain parts of my experience remain stable".

The other common situation is that of sleep, where the infant has to experience the temporary separation from the parent and the reinforcement which comes upon awakening to find the parent still there. This repetition eventually leads to the notion that reassures to the baby "I can be asleep for a while and count on the fact that my parent will be there when I wake up".

The last point is that this energy connection between all members of the family has continuous effects on the baby and can be used by parents to their advantage. What do I mean by this? Since energy exchanges in both directions, parents can send or broadcast information to the baby as this is happening automatically anyway. By 'broadcast', I mean the parent can simply send thoughts, feelings or words with the intention of their child picking up on these signals. If this remains outside of the parents' consciousness, they will not make any effort to use this pathway of communication and will instead allow "default settings" to take over. This can be deleterious for many reasons, but the most serious is sending an unintended message, including both statements and emotions, which the baby has no way to put into proper perspective.

An example of this is a distraught mother who inadvertently sends the baby the energetic signal through her own thought that says "something must be wrong with my baby because she cries all the time and can't sleep, I don't know what to do, I am fearful." This message will be interpreted by the immature baby's nervous system as: "Emergency! My foundation and source of energy and sustenance is expressing her fear in this moment! I'd better not let my guard down, and certainly I'd better not fall asleep because something terrible may happen or I may be separated from my source forever! I must cry as loudly as possible to maintain my vital connection and keep her close by..." As you can see, this message is not even close to what's really happening, but it is interpreted as such because of the immaturity of the infant's nervous system and the understandable lack of life experience, coupled with the energy influences.

I often tell parents to use this connection by sending thoughts of calm, acceptance and understanding, followed by what I like to call "foreshadowing". This technique is one where the parent can project through thought or spoken phrases an acknowledgement of the baby's current predicament and then lead them to what the parent's expectation is in the near future.

An example is, the parent thinks or says out loud, "I know you are not able to do things on your own yet, but I am confident in the near future you'll know how to calm yourself and sleep with ease." Just by projecting the feeling and energy associated with this theme, the parent can give the baby the imprint or pathway to follow according to their expectation.

Another way to go about it would be to say to another family member in person or on the phone while in the baby's presence, "I wonder how quickly my baby will learn how to sleep or calm himself?" Or even more open-ended might be, "I wonder what new skills and accomplishments my baby will attain in the next 2 weeks or months?"

These statements serve to send the energy associated with them to the baby as they are initiated and projected from the parent to them. Thus, more positive influences are carried along the energetic pathway which the baby is utilizing already. This technique can be useful throughout

childhood and for many different scenarios.

Newborn Infants

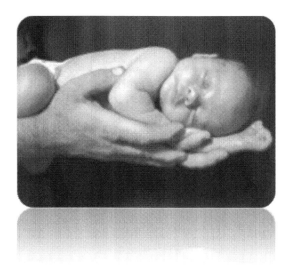

In my practice, I always look forward to seeing a new mother and her young baby. This is a great opportunity to assist in charting the course for the child's upbringing. Not that everything can be predicted, or that someone's life experience can be chosen. It's just that awareness and knowledge of what's happening to a baby at certain stages of development is so important to understanding how to handle the age appropriate issues that will come up later. And when a new mother is prepared for the changes and challenges, the baby's experience is much less stressful.

Let's take the scenario where a young baby is fussy, colicky, "high maintenance", sleep reversed, etc. This is one of the most trying times for parents and baby alike. For the parents and pediatrician, the questions begin... Is it gas? Breast milk? Allergies? Something the mother is eating? Constipation? Although this line of questioning has merits, it is too limiting. This view only acknowledges physical reasons for these behaviors when there are very real non-physical, energetic influences that can account for these same problems. Are we to assume there must be a physical reason and a physical reason only for a baby's condition? I don't think so.

After years of seeing babies and parents, I have been able to use my understanding of both energy medicine and conventional medicine, to assess, explain, and treat complex issues in newborns. In my clinical practice, I use a broad application of energy medicine principles to look beyond physical causes and even beyond the baby's physical body and individual energy system in order to understand and provide effective treatments.

In the newborn or young baby, I have found that history plays a very important role. The most important components are:

1) Prenatal influences and

2) Family history influences

Both of these areas are tremendously impacted by the mother's status before, during, and after the pregnancy.

It is not hard to understand a mother's worry if she has had prior problems during pregnancy or a previous miscarriage. These feelings and worries are unavoidable and expected. What we have not understood until now is the impact the mother's thoughts, feelings, and overall energy pattern have on the baby, even in the prenatal time period.

I like to say that this time for the baby is one in which they are "introduced" to the world experience through the mother's experience. I don't see any way that the baby can possibly be shielded from experiencing what the mother experiences. Nor do I think it would be healthy to do so. But an overall awareness of this connection can make a tremendous difference in the baby's ability to adjust to inevitable changes and thus better maintain a balanced physical, mental, and emotional status.

The other obvious component at work here is the immaturity of the baby's nervous system. This will cause over-reactions, imprinting of patterns and associations and nervous system correlations that can be inefficient and problematic.

Let's take a simple example of a pregnant mother on the 4th of July. She is enjoying a gathering in the backyard when suddenly a loud firecracker goes off in the neighbor's yard. She jumps, is startled, and her heart starts to race. This lasts for about 30 seconds and then her heart rate (and sympathetic nervous system responses) returns to normal.

What has the baby, who is now 8 months gestational age, experienced? The ability to hear, feel, move and appreciate any and all effects on the mother is well developed and fully functional. We can surmise that the baby also was startled, maybe had an increased heart rate as well, but most importantly, the baby would interpret this episode as a threat to the mother's safety. Even though we know, and the mother knows, firecrackers and the noise they make are not a direct threat, the baby has no way to differentiate this fact from what he/she experiences and feels through the mother. This, then, is a set up for an "imprint", which can become reinforced with later similar sounds and experiences.

Once the baby is born, all it takes is for a few loud noise episodes to solidify the theme or notion to the baby and growing child, "Loud noises are scary, a threat to myself and my security (the mother), and I'd better be ready for any loud noise to occur unexpectedly, on any given day and in any time frame."

Obviously, one can see how inefficient and prone to expending too much energy this scenario can cause. This can lead to less energy being available to the baby for age appropriate adjustments and compensation for things like gas and indigestion, feelings of being alone or abandoned, and sleep issues. It is not the fault of mother or baby; it is just the baby's interpretation of these circumstantial experiences that cause this outcome.

What I have found as a physician who sees babies, kids and parents, is that once parents know about these influences, they can take steps to remedy these imprints. I use The BodyTalk System along with Chinese medicine principles and point stimulation techniques to address and correct these problems in babies. Many of the same energy balancing techniques that I use in my office can be learned and safely applied by the parents at home.

If the baby receives the right signals and interprets these correctly, the energy pattern can be updated to suit the current environment and situation. Basically, we're talking about reassurance to the baby's system that "all is well", and that there is no need to over-react to triggers or stimuli that previously may have been perceived as dangerous or life threatening. We might also describe this as accelerated learning, or catch-up learning, helping the child's system to operate with the age-appropriate settings most beneficial for their stage of development.

Commonly, the BodyTalk session with a pregnant mom will involve certain links or tapping protocols for the baby and certain ones for the mother. Since each case is unique, we go into the session with no particular focus or agenda. Rather the intention is to provide assistance to the ongoing healing processes which are always active.

Physiological links for the baby are common at certain stages of the pregnancy and preparation links are often beneficial for the mother as her body gets ready for the birth process. These are examples of situations that are obvious and can be easily prepared for. However, there can be other influences that one might not think are relevant or important, and these are the categories which The BodyTalk System can help us to address and focus on. These might be family history influences from either side of the family tree, previous events in the mother's experience (like miscarriages or difficult labor and deliveries), moving to another part of the country while pregnant, and any other stressor on the family system the baby is about to be born into. As you can see, this opens up a whole new vista when it comes to influences that require energy from the baby and the mother to deal with.

One of the foundational principles of any treatment system is that the sooner one intervenes to correct a problem the easier it is to resolve. This makes the prenatal period a golden opportunity to prevent these imprint experiences from causing problems later on in the child's life. My experience in doing BodyTalk treatments with this group of mothers has taught me how individual each case is and how numerous the influences can be on both mother and baby.

When seeing newborns and young babies, we are always reverting back to the prenatal time period and early influences that the baby experiences. Letting parents know that the energy medicine system can help to explain their baby's behavior is the most useful aspect of this style of practice for me.

Toddlers

Once babies progress beyond the newborn period and become mobile, their whole outlook shifts once again. There is now a dynamic pull between wanting to do things individually as a toddler and wanting to stay in the comfortable and familiar role of "baby". I think parents can do a lot to foreshadow what's in store for their little ones by using the age appropriate energy medicine techniques mentioned above.

Applying energy medicine principles is a wonderful way to guide the toddler's system as it undergoes major dynamic shifts on a daily basis. The BodyTalk System operates with the premise that the child's innate wisdom is constantly reorganizing and arranging itself to distribute energy in order of priority. My view is that one of the best uses of The BodyTalk System is to highlight for the child (and family) what exactly is on that priority list in the moment. This way, conscious focus can be utilized by all concerned for the benefit of the child.

For example, let's say a 3 year old has just become an older brother to a newborn sister. We have to recognize that he will put this new arrival in his own context according to his current level of understanding. He might think this younger sibling is only a temporary phenomenon and tolerate her for a short time or he may react right away.

Emotional upheaval is common in this age group, not because the system wants to feel frustrated, but because the process of change is happening so fast. From an energy perspective there needs to be an emotional "pop off valve" that serves to release some of the pressure caused by this life changing event. Once again, the immaturity of the nervous system makes it difficult for the toddler to give up the "baby" programs he has come to know and love his whole lifetime. Only in rare circumstances or with plenty of "foreshadowing" as mentioned above by the parents will he accept the baby from the beginning along with his new role as big brother.

Another factor I like to bring up in consultations with parents of kids in this toddler age group is what I'll call their underlying program of individuality. I believe that one of the main themes or programs a child is born with is the statement, "I must become an individual, expressing myself in my own individual way!". This manifests in the form of constantly saying "No!", testing of boundaries and limits, and the exertion of personal will power in all its glory. If these behaviors can be understood by parents for what they are, expressions of this underlying program which is desirable in the long run, then the short term tolerance of the tantrums and unreasonable demands can be dealt with on a higher level of understanding.

One of the characteristics of toddlers is that they absorb information like a sponge, and therefore I will often recommend that parents use this to their advantage. Third party interactions are particularly useful, because by the time the child is three or four, they have become desensitized to interactions occurring in their own household.

A common scenario conducive to the foreshadowing technique would go like this;

> The mother is on the phone with grandma and the toddler is within earshot. The mother says something like, "I'll bet Johnny will be sleeping on his own by the time he turns four. He already knows some of the letters of the alphabet. I wonder what new things he'll be doing when he starts preschool..."

By making these statements, the mother is expressing her expectations as well as complimenting him indirectly through the phone conversation. This removes her from being in a demanding role, and simply expresses her desire to know if and when he will accomplish the next stages of his development. This will encourage the child to express his individuality without feeling the need to struggle against the mother (and other family members) who symbolize the family structure, which his developing nervous system may classify as rigid and unchangeable, especially his role in it, "the toddler-older brother".

Another really important milestone to foreshadow is the impending start of school. I cannot emphasize enough the amount of preventative preparation that can be done just by laying the groundwork for upcoming changes in the near future for your child. As mentioned earlier, broadcasting thoughts, feelings, statements, and expectations to your child can help immensely in the months and years leading up to the beginning of school. Now the toddler can see his or her changing role going from "the toddler-older brother" to the "kindergartener-explorer of the school territory".

You as the parent can use any imagery or descriptions that you want. For example, you might describe how neat it will be to ride the bus, meet the new teacher and other students, play outside at recess, etc. Using their 5th birthday as a milestone foreshadowing their readiness for school can be talked about many months in advance, building anticipation and eagerness. Your child will pick up on this mostly through the feelings you are projecting about the excitement, accomplishment and pride you will have in your youngster when that special day arrives: the first day of school.

Remember to check in with your own recollection of your experience when you started school, and take active steps to control any negative energy connotations that your child may inadvertently absorb from your experience in an age reciprocal resonance kind of way (see *Energy Medicine Principle #5: Resonance*).

The Family Matrix

> *"The family matrix is a very important group that the BodyTalk practitioner will need to address often... The family matrix is designed to be a healthy, nurturing, spiritual, and protective dynamic that is very important for good health."*
>
> - Excerpt from *The BodyTalk System* by John Veltheim, Module 9, 3rd edition, 2003

Before moving on to the school age category, I'd like to discuss the BodyTalk concept of the family matrix and the pivotal role it plays in all aspects of pediatrics. I have found that as a pediatrician, this category comes up in BodyTalk sessions the most for my patients and families and in retrospect; I can now say it is no surprise.

We live in energy matrix frameworks all the time, be they in our homes, jobs, extended families, sports teams, etc. An energy matrix is the concept or pattern that makes up a social structure or culture. You will have a family matrix or energetic structure that you grew up in as the child, and the family matrix you are in now as the parent.

The family matrix has particular importance because it is the first group matrix we are born into, and it serves as the template upon which all other matrices we experience will be compared and evaluated against. We are all familiar with the concept of parental bonding and how important it is in those first few days and weeks after birth. The energy correlations with this relationship with one's parents are far-reaching and lifelong. Because of the rapid changes a child experiences through their early years, this relationship with the family matrix is also subject to changes and therefore requires flexibility and understanding.

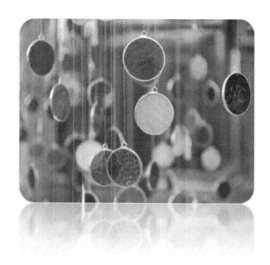

One of the images that John Bradshaw, author of *Bradshaw On: The Family*, uses to describe family dynamics is that of a mobile, where each individual family member is represented by a different object on a string. If one part of the mobile is touched or disturbed, the whole apparatus moves and alters its configuration as it seeks to rebalance. The family matrix is similar in that it seeks to maintain balance at all times as each of its members is subject to the influences that any one of them experiences.

Using the energy medicine paradigm has many advantages for describing reasons for illness and seemingly odd behaviors, and this is one instance where I find parents can gain the most as far as understanding the dynamics in their current family, in addition to the family matrix they grew up in.

101

To explain this further, we can look more specifically at the concept of "age reciprocal resonance". This resonance effect comes into play when the parent absorbs the energy broadcast coming from their own child. A child's experience of a particular age stimulates the parent's own (unconscious) memories, programs, experiences, emotions, etc., relating to when they were that age. This resonance can provoke some uncomfortable feelings that manifest as heightened anger, frustration, fear, and other emotions in the parent. These feelings are often interpreted as responses to the behavior of the child, resulting in countless appointments with doctors and professionals.

Rather than seeking treatment to "fix" the child's behavior, I have found that the ultimate solution is for the parent to examine their own history. When done with proper guidance and support, this has proven to be a wonderful opportunity for parents to revisit their own experiences at that age and seek resolution, acceptance, healing, understanding, and a different perspective now that the parent is older and wiser. Needless to say, when the parent does this kind of work on their own, the child's behavior problems seem to magically go away. Of course, we know that it isn't magic, but rather hard work and diligence on the part of the parent.

Age reciprocal resonance can also go in the opposite direction where parents have the ability to project their own experience or "unfinished business" onto their child. This is certainly not what a parent wants for their own child, but when it is an unconscious influence it happens regardless of what they want. The child is usually unaware of the details of what happened with their parents in the past and the child is also unaware of the outgoing energy expenditure that is being consumed trying to "deal with" the unresolved problems the parent had.

Hence, the more conscious and aware all members of a given family matrix are, the more ability they have to fine tune, prevent, and accentuate the positive. This is a very important point to remember, especially when one extrapolates back into the family tree on both parent's sides of the family.

These concepts and categories are accessible through The BodyTalk

System, and I cannot over emphasize how important this can be to help

explain, understand and treat difficult conditions in the pediatric age group.

School Age

Once kids are in school, their learning takes a quantum leap forward and includes social interaction, peer group influences, authority figures, routine changes, environment sensitivity, and the list goes on and on. Despite these changes, the still developing nervous system remains similar in its strategies of operation. Decisions must be made based on previous experience and the nervous system's current level of understanding.

This is an age where events and their consequences are stored with the emotional, mental, and physical impacts recorded at the time. Depending on the child's degree of sensitivity, compensatory shifts of energy, behavior, response, and the like, habitual settings are usually what end up being relied upon for coping. These can then be triggered to occur again and again.

> Memory is deceptive because it is colored by today's events.
>
> -Albert Einstein

Let's look at an example: An eight year old girl is comfortably riding the bus home from school. She suddenly notices a fight break out between two older boys, slugging each other in the next seat over from her. One of the boys has a bloody nose before the bus driver breaks it up and separates them. After arriving home, the girl is able to tell her mother what

 happened and the rest of the evening is uneventful. The next day she is terrified to get on the bus, and her mother drives her to school. She refuses to ride the bus for the next few weeks, and now her mother seeks out help to enable her daughter to get over this fear.

I am using this scenario to point out two important details.

First, the degree of sensitivity of some kids is such that even being in close proximity to events that don't affect them directly can have long lasting influences.

Second, the way the nervous system works in its recording function of events is much more involved than many parents realize.

Our central nervous system has the ability to record not just the visual and auditory components of events themselves, but also the trivial and miniscule bits of information that we normally are unaware of. For example, this child in the above vignette would likely have recorded not just the scene of the boys fighting on the bus, but the weather that day, the smell of the bus interior, the colors in her immediate surroundings, the clothes she was wearing, the bus drivers reaction and facial expressions, etc.

These triggers can be activated even far away from the original scene (on the school bus) and this is where anxiety and school phobias can become problematic. The BodyTalk System gives us a way to investigate what these triggers might be, long after the initiating event has taken place. Sometimes, the event is long forgotten or not known in the first place, and this is another situation where BodyTalk can be very helpful in uncovering the underlying issue.

School age is a wonderful time in a child's development. If your child is beyond the school age range already, think back to some of their experiences and ask yourself the question, "What might my child have experienced that could have a long lasting impact and "settings" associated with them even now?" I think this approach is the best way to prepare and prevent your child from expending energy unnecessarily or in an inefficient manner. You must continually help them to update their own "settings" so that they end up as teenagers and young adults with a balanced energy system optimized for their particular needs.

Teenagers

The teenage years can be difficult for all involved, but I believe a better

understanding of what the underlying motivations are of teenagers and

what they are trying to accomplish at that important stage of life is crucial to

a parent's preparation, endurance, and sanity.

If we look at the broader picture, a teenager is rapidly approaching

independence. Ideally, this is a gradual, step by step process, with increasing degrees of freedom and responsibility. Unfortunately, this rarely happens.

Let me explain...

According to the energy medicine system, we all have an internal program or directive that controls the timing of events (like puberty), our growth and development, learning stages, types of reasoning abilities, etc. Through research in anatomy, physiology, and biochemistry we know that the programming of these growth events are controlled primarily by the hormonal system in the body, called the endocrine system, and its interrelationship with the brain and entire nervous system.

At a deeper level, there is also an ongoing program within us during childhood and into adolescence that continuously pushes us towards independence. The body is very smart, and it knows we cannot make this shift from dependent child to independent young adult in one day.

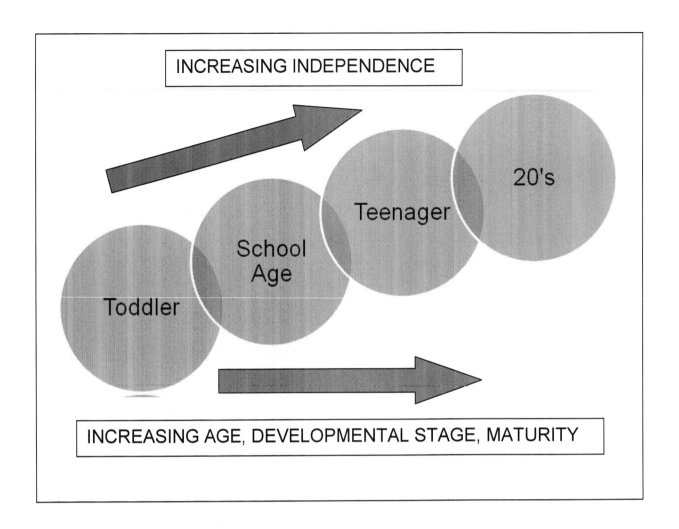

In fact, the process in my view starts in the toddler years, progresses

through the teenage years, and then culminates in the early twenties. So,

this is a long drawn out process. What many parents don't understand until

it's too late, is that this process needs to be nurtured throughout the whole

time period, not just in the last few years of adolescence. If this is not

done, then the teenager has no alternative but to express his or her

"independence" in often destructive and outwardly negative ways.

Even more complicating is the fact that this process occurs at varying rates and to varying degrees depending on the individual, the family culture, personalities, etc. In my opinion, the often described period of rebellion that most teenagers go through can be tempered by allowing age and maturity appropriate freedom in order to satisfy this ongoing internal program which says, "I must become an individual, I must become my own person". In an energy sense, this contradicts what the young person has grown up believing, particularly when it comes to the family matrix concept discussed earlier. The teenager realizes that the comfort and support that his family matrix has provided for all these years, will one day change and morph into a new relationship where he will still be a member of his family of origin, but his status will change from "active child member of the family", to "former child, now grown up and doing his own thing, member of the family". Eventually, he will assume the role of father, adult or parent in his own family matrix and his children will start the cycle all over again.

If a parent can maintain clarity on this issue over the course of the child's upbringing, then the teenage years can be made more tolerable and understandable to both kids and parents.

A comparison I like to offer parents is that of coaching. Have you ever seen a track coach compete in the very same race as his own athlete? Does a teacher take the same test as her students? Of course not! Likewise, parents should not put themselves in a competitive stance with their teenagers, but rather take the role of adviser or coach. In this way, you are on the same team but not competing against each other. I understand there is a fine balance to this, but with time and practice (as with anything else) progress can be made and a healthy relationship can be fostered.

To reiterate this important point, the process must take place gradually over time, not when the teenager reaches some predetermined age. Our body and internal system is designed to make changes slowly, not all of a sudden. If we can work in concert with the body's internal rhythms things tend to work out much better.

One other point I want to make is the concept of keeping oneself updated. This means reminding or reinforcing to yourself what stage your child is in, and what stage you are in as a parent. Here again, the energy medicine paradigm gives us a perspective within which we can interpret the nuances and changes in the teenager-parent relationship. It is quite common for a parent to operate with "settings" from 10 years ago, while the teenager is operating with "settings" more appropriate for someone in their twenties.

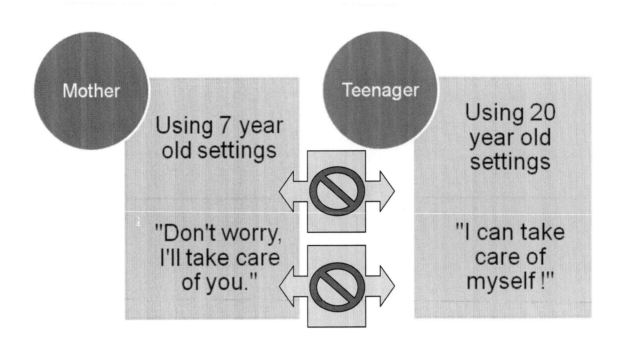

Do you see the discrepancy and the inevitable conflict? Of course, no parent will verbally say to their teenager, "I'm treating you the same way I did when you were 7", but the impact and the felt sense by the teenager will be there nonetheless. This is easily explainable by an energy medicine based interpretation. I have found over and over again that this is a real and common phenomenon.

Unfortunately for parents, this cannot be hidden from the teenagers themselves. Once they feel this pull back to an earlier time being expressed non-verbally by their parents, they will move full steam ahead to counteract it. This is an undesirable position for both parents and teenagers and the best solution is to prevent it from happening in the first place.

The only other alternative is to start from today, acknowledge the discrepancy between the two sides, and move forward with a new plan and goal to meet on common ground. If this can be done with both parents and teenagers engaged in their updated age appropriate settings, then improved relationships and a smoother transition to adulthood can result.

"People are like stained-glass windows. They sparkle and shine when the sun is out, but when the darkness sets in, their true beauty is revealed only if there is a light from within".

-Elizabeth Kubler Ross

How do we put all this altogether? You now know the energy principles explained in Part I, and The BodyTalk System as a modality discussed in Part II, as well as the age range correlations in Part III. In this final section, I want to give you 3 case studies where you can "look over my shoulder", as I assess and treat these children and parents. I want to give you some insight into how I evaluate and interpret what is going on with my patients. Please be advised that these are given as educational examples only, and should not be taken as specifically meant for your child in any way, even if your child happens to have the same symptom or condition described in the vignettes.

Case #1: 5 month old baby with colic

This baby girl (I will call her Courtney) presented at 5 months of age with

the mother stating she had been a fussy baby since birth. Her symptoms

consisted of gassiness and indigestion, spitting up during and after

feedings, crying and screaming episodes and poor sleep. Her mother

described her as being unhappy about 90% of the time.

The mother's initial comment was, "All I've been told so far is that she

needs to grow out of it. I'm hoping more can be done."

Courtney is the first baby for this married couple. Her current history

reveals that she breast feeds well, has gained appropriate weight, and

other than some upper respiratory congestion she does not have any

significant developmental or medical problems.

The mother's pregnancy with her was complicated by hyperemesis

gravidum (excessive nausea and vomiting) with weight loss which required

hospitalization and treatment with intravenous fluids on multiple occasions.

Around 35 weeks gestation, the mother developed preeclampsia (high blood pressure) and despite treatment she needed to have labor induced at 37 weeks gestation. After 25 hours of labor a C-section was performed and Courtney made her entrance into the world.

BodyTalk is a great modality to start a treatment session because it gives important information about what the child's system is already focusing and working on. It did not take long for it to become apparent that specific body systems needed to be re-focused and balanced and connected.

The first link or category that came up for Courtney was primary matrix linking with the father's energy system. This is quite common and shows how important both parents are to the balance and stability of the baby's energy system. I gently tapped the top of the head and the middle of the chest to give the tactile and energetic input for Courtney's system to register and work on this first category.

The second link was an active memory defragmentation of the experience of the last 24 hours prior to Courtney's birth, namely the time of labor for the mother and the birth experience by C-section. Active memory defragmentation means we focus on this event and encourage Courtney's

system to process and neutralize the impact of that experience so that the

minimum amount of energy is expended. This allows her to move on and

progress through her current stage of development without having to

devote extra energy on the past event of her stressful birth experience.

In addition to these two BodyTalk tapping protocols, I applied an essential

oil blend to the bottoms of her feet for balancing and relaxation, and I used

a *Colorpuncture* light set to stroke specific meridian lines on the baby's feet

called 'Prenatal Lines'. This light technique applied to 3 lines on each foot

invokes the remembrance of the baby's prenatal energy settings, triggering

a connection to her underlying individual blueprint that she can refer back

to for the purpose of balancing and nourishing her own system.

In addition to the hands on treatment of Courtney, I spent quite a bit of time

describing different things that the mother could do at home using her own

intuition and energy system to influence her baby's daily experience. I saw

Courtney for 2 follow up visits and used the same modalities but with

different protocols. Within a few weeks Courtney had attained a new level of calm. Her parents were pleased with the changes and were confident that she could now do well on her own.

My experience with young babies indicates that they tend to respond very quickly and seem to need only a little outside stimulation to encourage their systems to get back on track. Of course, the growing awareness and understanding of the parents correlates directly as well with the baby's sense of security, confidence, and emerging individuality. This case was very instructive in that it showed how important the experience of the birth process is to a young baby, even more so than what is going on in their current environment and daily routine.

Case #2: 6 year old with severe eczema.

This young boy, I'll call him Paul, had severe, chronic eczema (an intensely itchy and sometimes painful skin disorder) that affected various parts of his body, most notably his hands and fingers, elbows, knees, low back and buttocks, and feet. According to his mother, he started to have skin trouble around 1 year of age. Ever since then it has been a constant battle to keep his skin from flaring up and to control itching especially at night.

Over the years the parents had tried food elimination diets, allergy testing, bath soaks, various over the counter anti-itch creams and prescription topical medications. He needed to wear band aids to cover open sore areas on his hands during the day, and at night he wore full sleeves, pants and socks or gloves on his hands to minimize itching and picking at his skin during the night.

Paul's past history was otherwise unremarkable; he had never been hospitalized nor had surgery. His mother could not recall him ever having to be on antibiotics for anything other than skin infections. Paul's father also has eczema but not as severe. His mother stated that he tends to feel

hot most of the time and he can have episodes where he worries a lot.

Paul has had stomachaches in the past and also has mild lactose

intolerance.

For his first treatment, we started with BodyTalk and the first link was

balancing of the midline energy centers (or chakras) with the endocrine

system. This combination is common in growing children and signifies the

importance of energy distribution through the chakra system and timing of

hormonal regulation through the endocrine system. These are both

processes that are happening all the time. The tapping process simply

calls the attention of the child's system to this fact and promotes more

clarity and efficiency according to the child's own schedule and order of

priority. This is one of the most important facets of the BodyTalk System;

we are not trying to force anything, we are just enhancing the internal

workings of the child's rebalancing already in progress.

The second BodyTalk link was family history on father's side linking to

Paul's general body energy system. This is what can be called an inherited predisposition which might be taking up more of his energy than need be. In this case, we focus on decreasing that influence so as to free up more of Paul's energy to be used in other more important functions (like normal growth and development).

The third link matched the left right brain balancing protocol called cortices with the spleen organ and energy sub circuit system. This correlation is important from a Chinese medicine point of view because the spleen energy is in charge of nourishing the digestive, respiratory, and skin systems of the body. Here again, we just highlight through focus and tapping to direct the child's energy system to pay attention and make adjustments where needed.

In addition to BodyTalk, I used essential oils on Paul's feet, *Colorpuncture* light on various point locations to strengthen the digestive system, and I used tuning forks to apply vibration to acupuncture points on the spleen, lung, and stomach meridians. I also used infrared light treatments and oral natural detoxification supplements.

After about 6 months of seeing him twice a month, his eczema had improved significantly and the areas of involvement had localized to just the low back and buttock areas. His mother remarked that his skin was in the best condition they had seen it in the past several years.

Case #3: 11 year old boy with Crohn's Disease

"Roger" is an 11 year old with Crohn's disease which was just diagnosed a few months prior to his first visit with me. According to his parents he had a colonoscopy which showed involvement of the terminal ileum (a part of the small intestine) with the typical findings consistent with inflammatory bowel disease or Crohn's. His past medical history was essentially unremarkable. He had no previous hospitalizations or surgeries. His mother recalled him being a pretty healthy baby with no significant illnesses and normal development. Roger is the youngest of three children and lives in a stable home and does well in school.

Roger is described by his mother as a sensitive child compared to her other two older kids. His main symptom was crampy abdominal pain which was present most of the day and self described as between 3-5 out of 10 on a pain scale. He had been started on two medications for the Crohn's since the time of his diagnosis but the pains had persisted.

After spending an hour with Roger and his parents discussing his history and the modalities available to try, we decided to use non-invasive modalities only. Roger definitely did not want needles of any kind, so we started with BodyTalk, essential oils, *Colorpuncture,* and tuning forks.

The first BodyTalk links were large intestine linking with the 2nd chakra (which is below the navel) linking with the process of lymphatic drainage from the pelvis. This was followed by cortices linking with the small intestine to encourage balance between the central nervous system and the nerve networks surrounding the small intestine itself. The third tapping protocol was spleen linking with the earth element (from the Chinese medicine principle of 5 elements balancing the internal organs) which is a way to mobilize more energy into the digestive system circuit. Colorpuncture points were used on the abdomen, in the midline and on the forehead, and an essential oil blend specific for strengthening the digestive system was used on the bottoms of the feet.

We continued treatments every 2-3 weeks and by the 6th treatment he was able to go most days with 0 or 1 out of 10 on the pain scale. Over the next

1 to 2 years Roger had intermittent episodes of mild abdominal pains and loose stools every few months or so, but he was able to keep up with school work and other activities.

It has been more than 5 years since I first saw Roger and he is 17 years old now. A couple of years ago he agreed to try acupuncture with needles and we have added that to his maintenance regimen. I now see him only once every few months and he has continued to do very well.

One of the side effects of inflammatory bowel disease is poor growth and development because the disease prevents proper absorption of food and nutrients through the digestive system. This is compounded by the disease diverting energy that should be devoted to fulfilling the requirements of normal growth and development. In addition, it is common for patients with Crohn's disease to need steroid medications which can also adversely affect their growth.

I'm happy to report that Roger is almost 6 feet tall and an avid basketball player and fan. He has not needed any medications in recent years and I expect his status to continue to improve as he grows into adulthood. With this many years of experience, Roger will always know that he can rely on these methods to help his body and underlying system stay in good shape no matter what challenges await him in the future.

Final thoughts

I have shared with you the most important things I want you (and all parents) to know about your kids from an energy medicine perspective. I have related my philosophy of how energy medicine can help us to understand the dynamic interactions that all children experience as they go through the normal stages of growth and development. Hopefully you now have a better understanding of how energy medicine can play a significant role as a preventive medicine modality as well as an acute treatment option to address illness, injury, and other imbalances.

I believe energy medicine complements conventional medicine without competing with or negating its important role in the health care of children. I do however believe that we should not rely entirely on the conventional medical model. Energy medicine offers a non-invasive treatment system that in my experience is very effective for children.

One of the things you may hear conventionally trained MDs say about alternative or energetic medicine is that there isn't any valid research to prove that it works. (I know because I used to think that way!) So I want to share a few of my thoughts about the topic of "evidence based medicine", which is very strongly entrenched in the western medical mindset.

"Reality based medicine"

Nowadays we hear about the importance of evidence based medicine. I believe this is an attempt by our collective left brain to hold on to its position it has held over the last couple centuries. Even when there is "evidence" in other scientific fields like physics, the medical establishment refuses to accept the notion that we as human beings are much more than physical beings. We are composed of numerous energy fields, many of which can be demonstrated and viewed with the instruments available today.

"Reality Based Medicine"

I propose a new term called "reality based medicine" in order to more accurately describe what's really happening in and around us as human beings. If one of the smallest known components of our universe is the atom (I won't get into subatomic particles) and we know that an atom can "appear" as either a particle or a wave, then we as human beings must also have this characteristic of dual appearance as particle and wave. Is this not logical?

The energy medicine paradigm allows for this and in fact embraces it as part of its foundational principle, which is that we are energetic beings. All of the "alternative medicine" systems incorporate this energy component in one form or another. Isn't it time that we as physicians caught up with the rest of the world?

My main criticism of "evidence based medicine" is the fact that the main supposition is that we are all the same. Of course, everyone knows this is not true. So how can smart people like doctors and researchers make this error? I believe it comes from microfocusing on what can be proven statistically at the expense of what can be incorporated realistically by everyday people. It's one thing to say a certain medication is good for your heart, it's quite another to say that same medication is going to force your body to do something it was never designed to do. This is one of the greatest pitfalls of modern medicine. I believe if people have more complete information about what's going on in their bodies and the consequences of only following the evidence based medicine route, they

will be able to make more sound decisions for their own individual situation.

This can be further illustrated if we look at the example of how a child

learns. It is well known that kids learn differently. Some are more visual,

some auditory, some kinesthetic or feeling oriented, and this influences

how they are best able to learn.

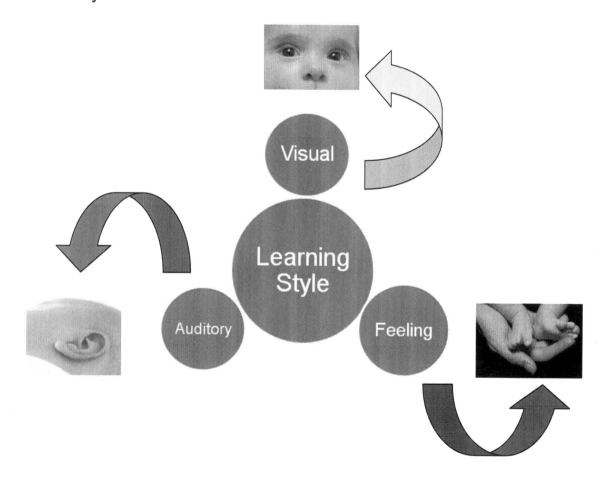

As a practicing physician in pediatrics, I have seen countless examples of

all three. Would it make sense to make all kids conform to learning in one way only? Of course not. Then why would we allow the same strategy to reign in the field of medicine? It doesn't make sense. We should be striving to individualize treatments, not designing 1 protocol and expect it to fit everyone.

Another example to illustrate this point is found in music. Could any of us imagine if only one form of music was considered acceptable, while all the other genres were excluded? This would never fly in our society where choice is so highly revered. And yet, in the world of medicine, we stick to conformity and accept what we hear on television. They tell us, if we have a certain condition, the best and only way to treat it is to take the next greatest medication on the market. How many times have these medications ended up harming significant portions of the population because of side effects (either known or unknown)? To me, this is evidence of what can happen when the mistaken assumption is made that when something is good for some it must be good for all.

I am constantly made aware of how symptom oriented our society is. We are so fixated on naming syndromes and diseases that we'll even make some up to sound good on commercials and thereby draw in people looking for an answer to their problem. I'm not saying these are not real conditions but I am questioning why a description of one or a collection of symptoms is elevated to the status of a disorder or disease. I think this is very misleading and should not be tolerated. It simply obscures the underlying causative issue and delays the proper treatment, or in the worst case scenario leads to the lifelong postponement of even addressing or finding out what the underlying cause is. I don't think most people would elect to do this if they were given proper and complete information from the outset.

I have learned through my clinical experience and my own study of energy medicine principles that this huge missing piece of the puzzle cannot be kept from the public any longer. It is simply too easy to get this information now. I believe we as physicians owe it to our patients to let them know they have a choice. And the choice is to encourage them to explore their own questions on health, using their own body as a living laboratory, not the statistics of the next research study in the newspaper or on the nightly news.

Finally, I admit that I must accept a dose of my own medicine. That is, while I may think a certain way about the need for choice when it comes to our own healthcare, I also acknowledge that there will be some people who make the choice to follow the conventional approach and only choose those treatments that have been "proven" in research studies. I respect and honor that choice, whether or not it has been arrived at with the full knowledge of the alternatives, the consequences, and the existence of differing opinions.

Two Statements to Remember

I want to conclude by leaving you with the following two statements:

"No one knows your child better than you do."

As practitioners, we are limited in what we can offer and how much

influence we have over you and your child. You are the most valuable ally

your child has, period. I applaud you for taking the time to educate yourself

on behalf of your child. I encourage you to explore many different sources

of information, all the while looking for consistency and concurrence among different authors and different fields of study. In my opinion, this is the surest way to find quality information that has stood the test of time.

"Your child is a work of art."

I think we have to remind ourselves that you and your children are living works of art, not physical robots in need of mechanical repairs. We must constantly explore the limits of our scientific understanding and attempt to go even further than what is currently explainable. I feel we owe this to you as your practitioners, you owe it to your kids as their parents, and your kids will have the responsibility to pass it on to their succeeding generations.

It is my hope that this has been helpful to those of you who are looking for a different perspective on your child's health and well-being. With the limitations of time and space, it is very likely that I will never speak to you or meet with you in person. However, I believe that your continued learning and quest for knowledge will be a model for your own children to follow, and this will serve to continue the process and further broaden their understanding of who they are.

What You Can Do For Your Child Right Now!

Many of the parents I see are highly motivated to start helping their children right away. Sometimes it is due to a serious illness, diagnosis, or disease, and other times they simply want to prevent any health or behavior problems from arising. Whatever situation you are in, you may find one or all of the following energy medicine techniques or options to be beneficial.

1. Start doing "Cortices" on your child today.

This is a simple and extremely effective BodyTalk tapping technique that can be done on your child everyday. It can be used for yourself, your kids, and other family members and friends to help reestablish a healthy balance of the brain and nervous system. If your child is old enough you can even teach your child to do it on him or herself. To learn this technique, just click on this link which takes you to the cortices video on my website.

http://www.principlesforparents.com/empfp-bodytalk

The video on this page features the founder of the BodyTalk System, Dr. John Veltheim, describing and demonstrating this technique. Listen for his experience with parents and their children!

2. Register for my live teleseminars and webinars.

There is no way I could possibly include all the information there is about energy medicine in one ebook, so I have (at the request of parents) decided to provide additional information on a variety of topics by way of teleseminars and webinars (online seminars). To see a list of topics and to register, go to   http://www.principlesforparents.com/empfp-webinars

3. Schedule a one-on-one consultation with me.

As I have stated before, every child is unique. Although I believe this book helps to give you direction on how to address the individual needs of your child, nothing takes the place of a one-on-one consultation where we can really delve into your child's specific situation. If you feel a consultation would be beneficial to you, we can schedule one over the phone. Please go to my website to read more about the advantages of an individualized consultation: http://www.principlesforparents.com/empfp-consultation

4. Schedule an appointment to see me in person.

If you live in the Portland, Oregon or Southwest Washington areas and you're interested in seeing me for an office visit consultation, call my receptionist at 360-449-4500. Additionally, you can download the pediatric new patient forms from my clinic website here:

http://www.principlesforparents.com/empfp-clinic-scheduling

Be sure to read my Welcome Letter to Parents. It will give you a clear idea of what to expect as we work together using energy medicine principles and techniques for the benefit of your child and entire family.

5. Schedule an appointment with a BodyTalk practitioner.

The International BodyTalk Association regulates the training and certification of all its practitioners. They have a list of all the certified practitioners all over the world. You can search to find one by your state or zip code by going to the 'Find a Practitioner' section of the IBA here:

http://www.bodytalksystem.com

6. Investigate energy medicine resources.

Although I am a big believer in BodyTalk, Chinese medicine, and other holistic methods of healing, there are many others that are safe and effective. Do your 'due diligence' in investigating the methods and practitioners that you choose to use for your child's health and well being. I have listed some of my favorite energy medicine resources here:

http://www.principlesforparents.com/empfp-to-resources

7. Sign up for my Principles for Parents Newsletter:

http://www.principlesforparents.com/empfp-home

8. Let your voice be heard!

I am always learning from the parents and children I am so fortunate to treat and consult with. Even if we may never interact directly, please know that I appreciate your feedback and comments. You can post your thoughts on my blog at: http:www.principlesforparents.com/empfp-blog

A Special Thank You

I would like to extend my sincerest gratitude to you for reading this book and exploring the energy medicine world on behalf of your child. By learning about the energy medicine principles, the BodyTalk system, the age range correlations with energy medicine, and by reading a few case study examples, you have now embarked upon your own journey of discovery.

In keeping with the philosophy of what I have put forth in this book, there is no one absolute way for you to proceed. You must navigate your own course and find what is right for you. You must resist the collective tendency toward conformity and categorization. Your child deserves more individual treatment than that.

If you are drawn to other modalities elsewhere, then I encourage you to go down that path. If you are inclined to seek out further treatments in accordance with my experience, please feel free to contact me. I stand ready to help you in any way I can.

I wish you all the best,

Peter Hanfileti, MD

Glossary of Terms

Age Reciprocal Resonance – this describes the energy relationship between your child's current age related experience and your experience when you were that age in your own childhood.

BodyTalk – the energy medicine modality I use for children in my practice involving kinesiology and tapping protocols to promote balancing of your child's system.

Chinese Medicine – this is a vast subject which includes the fields of acupuncture, herbal medicine, therapeutic exercise, diet and nutrition; it is truly a stand alone system and provides a framework which, in my opinion, is very useful in the description and evaluation of children.

Colic – the common condition in babies where irritability, crying, and fussiness happens for no clearly discernible reason.

Conservation – the principle of energy medicine which says your child's energy system sets up "savings accounts" to be prepared for potential repetition of events, and thereby conserve and protect itself.

Distribution – the principle of energy medicine which shows how your child's system distributes its energy among the many subsystems in charge of the physical, mental, emotional and spiritual categories of function.

Energy – the common currency among all disciplines which is vibrational in nature and essential for life and your child's wellbeing.

Family Matrix – the energy pattern or arrangement of a particular family unit which includes all members of that family (including pets).

Harmony – the principle of energy medicine which states that harmony and balance is a characteristic that your child's system strives for continuously.

Hierarchy – the principle of energy medicine that visually is represented by an ordered list where energy is expended according to priority, from most to least important.

Intelligence – the principle of energy medicine that makes the presumption that there is an underlying intelligence operating within and for your child's energy system.

Imprinting – this energy medicine principle describes the process by which experiences and events are categorized and memorized by your child's system.

Neuro-Linguistic Programming – also known as NLP, a fascinating modality which focuses on word choices and how we are affected by verbal conditioning, both consciously and unconsciously.

Resonance – this principle of energy medicine describes the vibrational nature of energy and how it can be picked up and propagated and even transferred to others.

Time Independence – this principle of energy medicine permits the effects of energy influences to be outside the confines of time. This is where 'settings' can become stuck and persist despite the triggering event having occurred in the distant past.

Settings – this term is used to characterize how a person holds their energy distribution pattern, in aspects of both quantity and quality.

Space Independence – this principle of energy medicine denotes how energy effects are felt and have their influence regardless of a person's location in space relative to another person. This is particularly true of parents and young children.

Ubiquity – this principle of energy medicine simply means that energy is everywhere, in many different forms, at all times.

Made in the USA
Lexington, KY
11 July 2011